# ENGLAND'S HEROES

## The essential guide to the stars of England's World Cup 2006 squad

*p*

This is a Parragon Book
First Published in 2006

Parragon
Queen Street House
4 Queen Street
Bath BA1 1HE, UK

ISBN 1-40547-188-3

The contents of this book are believed correct
at the time of printing. The publisher cannot
be held responsible for any errors, omissions
or changes, in the information contained therein.

All statistics are correct up to 1 January 2006.

A copy of the CIP data for this book is available
from the British Library upon request.

For Butler and Tanner
Writers: Julian Flanders and Adrian Besley
Project Editor: Julian Flanders
Designer: Craig Stevens

Photographs: Empics

Printed in China

# CONTENTS

## ENGLAND

Heroes or villains? 4

How they'll line up 6

Great match 6

Possible squad 7

Vital statistics 8

One to watch:
Shaun Wright-Phillips 8

Manager: Sven Goran-Eriksson 9

Route to the finals 9

## THE SQUAD

David Beckham 10

Wayne Rooney 12

John Terry 14

Frank Lampard 16

Michael Owen 18

Steven Gerrard 20

Joe Cole 21

Paul Robinson 22

Ashley Cole 23

Rio Ferdinand 24

Luke Young 25

Gary Neville 26

Sol Campbell 27

Ledley King 28

Jamie Carragher 29

### Other Squad Players

David James 30

Robert Green 30

Wayne Bridge 30

Paul Konchesky 30

Jermaine Jenas 31

Michael Carrick 31

Jermain Defoe 31

Peter Crouch 31

England's prospects 32

# ENGLAND

## HEROES OR VILLAINS?

**Some see England as certain finalists, others as potential failures. There's talent galore, but will that be enough to win football's most important competition?**

Whether it was misfortune – Rooney's injury and Ronaldinho's 'freak' goal – or tactical error, England will not want to repeat the disappointments of Japan and Korea or Euro 2004. If anything, the team has improved, with the emergence of John Terry and Ashley Cole as world-class defenders, the amazing progress of Lampard and the maturity – at least as a footballer – of Rooney. But the questions remain. How does Sven accommodate Gerrard, Beckham and Lampard in the midfield? Is Joe Cole the man to answer the long-standing left-side problem? And do England have the flexibility to change styles and formations to suit the match? If they can answer these questions, they could well come home as heroes.

**Above** For England to succeed in Germany much depends on the link-up play between Frank Lampard and captain David Beckham.

**Opposite** The time has come for the fast-maturing Joe Cole to prove that he can make it on the world stage.

### MORE QUESTIONS THAN ANSWERS

England's qualifying group looked pretty easy on paper, but somehow they managed to give the impression of struggling through. Sven kept faith with the team who had largely disappointed in Portugal, only really giving a chance to Paul Robinson (who took it) and Jermain Defoe (who didn't). England got off to a flyer – winning in Poland and in a tricky match against Wales – but defeat to Northern Ireland was a setback.

Added to a 1-4 friendly defeat against a mediocre Denmark, the result created tremors. England now had two must-win matches and sections of the press were already calling for Sven's head. They doubted his tactical sense, accused him of letting his captain, Beckham, run the team and claimed he played out-of-form players out of position. When Beckham was sent off in the penultimate match against Austria – the game looked up. But England held on for a 1-0 victory and as other results went their

In keeper Paul Robinson England have found the perfect replacement for David Seaman who retired from international football after the 2002 World Cup.

way, qualified with a game to spare. In the final match they enjoyed an impressive 2-1 victory over Poland. Everyone was heartened, but somehow the result merely underlined the existing questions.

## HOW THEY'LL LINE UP

Sven has been very loyal to his players and it seems unlikely he'll change his spots now. The spine of the team is settled and contains England's world beaters in Robinson, Lampard, Gerrard, Rooney and Michael Owen. Around them only the left-sided midfield postion looks up for grabs as Joe Cole still fails to look completely at home.

## GREAT MATCH

### 2002 ENGLAND 1-0 ARGENTINA

**WORLD CUP, GROUP STAGE**
**Sapporo Dome, Sapporo, Japan**

**England finally laid to rest** the Indian sign Argentina had held over them for 15 years with a determined and fantastically organized victory. Man-of-the match Nicky Butt put his Manchester United team-mate Veron in the shade, and Michael Owen provided a constant threat.

It was an early injury to Hargreaves that helped England gel. Sinclair replaced him and made inroads down the left and Scholes moved into the centre, where he drove the team forward. The goal came with just two minutes to go to half-time, Owen slipped around Pochettino, fell over his outstretched leg and referee Collina pointed to the spot. David Beckham, whose life had been made a misery after being sent-off in the 1998 match, took a deep breath, before hammering the ball past Cavallero.

Argentina camped themselves in England's half for the last 30 minutes of the game, but were frustrated by the midfield line and a brilliant Seaman save to deny Pochettino. Revenge was sweet – the blue-and-whites were all but boarding the plane home.

Injury or tactical manoeuvres could, however, lead to some interesting changes. England could utilise their strengths and play three at the back. A holding midfielder might provide a better mainspring for attack. And Sven might even consider switching to the

## POSSIBLE SQUAD

**Goalkeepers: Paul Robinson** (Tottenham Hotspur), **David James** (Manchester City), **Robert Green** (Norwich City)

**Defenders: Ashley Cole** (Arsenal), **Sol Campbell** (Arsenal), **Gary Neville** (Manchester United), **Rio Ferdinand** (Manchester United), **John Terry** (Chelsea), **Wayne Bridge** (Chelsea), **Luke Young** (Charlton Athletic), **Jamie Carragher** (Liverpool), **Ledley King** (Tottenham Hotspur)

**Midfielders: Steven Gerrard** (Liverpool), **David Beckham** (Real Madrid), **Joe Cole** (Chelsea), **Frank Lampard** (Chelsea), **Shaun Wright-Phillips** (Chelsea), **Jermaine Jenas** (Tottenham Hotspur), **Michael Carrick** (Tottenham Hotspur)

**Forwards: Wayne Rooney** (Manchester United), **Michael Owen** (Newcastle United), **Jermain Defoe** (Tottenham Hotspur), **Peter Crouch** (Liverpool)

*Back row (left to right): Ashley Cole, Rio Ferdinand, Jamie Carragher, Frank Lampard, Paul Robinson.*
*Front row: Wayne Rooney, Joe Cole, David Beckham, Steven Gerrard, Luke Young and Shaun Wright-Phillips.*

4-5-1 formation that Chelsea, Manchester United and others have used to great effect.

If such changes are employed there are a number of players waiting for their chance: Luke Young as a foraging full back; Ledley King, Michael Carrick or Jermaine Jenas in the midfield role and Shaun Wright-Phillips as a quick, skilful winger. Up front the tall Peter Crouch has shown he can offer something different, while Jermain Defoe could unleash his talent if he is given a run in the team.

### ONE TO WATCH
### Shaun Wright-Phillips

'I don't think he's the finished article yet, he can only get better.' Stuart Pearce's parting words on his young star implied Chelsea might have got the 21-year-old for a 'bargain' £21 million. In his few England appearances, Shaun has added to the argument, exhibiting a blistering turn of pace (he's the quickest at the club, claim Chelsea), great control and a

wicked shot. Bearing the tag of 'Ian Wright's adopted son' couldn't have been easy, particularly when Nottingham Forest let him go at 15 for being 'too small'. Switching to Manchester City, he soon impressed – on either flank and as a wing-back. Making his debut at 18, Shaun helped City into the Premier League and set about making his mark.

Premiership defenders soon discovered his twisting, turning runs to their cost. The 2003–04 campaign saw him bag 11 goals and make many more, forcing his price beyond the wallets of the chasing Liverpool and Arsenal: only Chelsea could afford him.

Shortly after arriving at Stamford Bridge in July 2005, Shaun marked his England debut with a superb solo goal. Suddenly, England had a new option: a lightning winger with the ability to beat defenders. It excited the fans and the media – but to accommodate Shaun would mean the unthinkable: dropping the captain. Barring a tactical rethink, Shaun

## VITAL STATISTICS

**WORLD RANKING** 9th
**KEEPER AND DEFENCE** 8/10
**MIDFIELD** 8/10
**ATTACK** 7/10
**STRENGTHS AND WEAKNESSES**
The nucleus of Eriksson's team has been together for two previous tournaments and know what is needed and what to expect. The defence will be tight and if Rooney comes alight, he could take the team a long way, if not they could struggle to score and go out with all too familiar limp performances.
**HOW FAR WILL THEY GO?**
If they can get over that elusive quarter-final hurdle, the doubts will disappear and they'll make the Final.

*Shaun Wright-Phillips exhibits the sort of skills that make him such an exciting prospect for club and country.*

goes to Germany as Beckham's understudy, but if he gets a chance, remember Psycho's words and don't be surprised to see a lot more of this youngster's stunning talent.

After the defeat to Northern Ireland, criticism of Sven's management style gathered momentum. True to character, he rode the flak and calmly led his team to the World Cup – but for the first time, the press seemed to have bruised him. The ice cold Swede now knows for sure, it's do or die in Germany.

*Sven-Goran Eriksson knows that Germany 2006 represents his last chance for glory with England.*

## COACH
### Sven Goran-Eriksson
(born 5 February 1948)
Record: P59 W34 D15 L10

The exact opposite of his predecessor Kevin Keegan, the Swede was a proven winner, a tactician rather than a motivator, unemotional and – for some, most controversially – a foreigner. Any initial outrage, though, was soon forgotten as Sven's tenure began well. Sven, and his assistant Tord Grip, brought their partnership – forged at Benfica and Lazio – to England and imposed their blueprint to great effect. Faithful to a 4-4-2 formation and reliant on pacy counter-attack, they built a reputation on loyalty to players and a calm response to victory or defeat.

### ROUTE TO THE FINALS

| DATE | | |
|---|---|---|
| 04.09.04 | AUSTRIA **2** | **2** ENGLAND |
| 08.09.04 | POLAND **1** | **2** ENGLAND |
| 09.10.04 | ENGLAND **2** | **0** WALES |
| 13.10.04 | AZERBAIJAN **0** | **1** ENGLAND |
| 26.03.05 | ENGLAND **4** | **0** NORTHERN IRELAND |
| 30.03.05 | ENGLAND **2** | **0** AZERBAIJAN |
| 03.09.05 | WALES **0** | **1** ENGLAND |
| 07.09.05 | NORTHERN IRELAND **1** | **0** ENGLAND |
| 08.10.05 | ENGLAND **1** | **0** AUSTRIA |
| 12.10.05 | ENGLAND **2** | **1** POLAND |

### EUROPEAN QUALIFYING GROUP 6 – FINAL TABLE

| TEAM | P | W | D | L | F | A | Pts |
|---|---|---|---|---|---|---|---|
| ENGLAND | 10 | 8 | 1 | 1 | 17 | 5 | **25** |
| POLAND | 10 | 8 | 0 | 2 | 27 | 9 | **24** |
| AUSTRIA | 10 | 4 | 3 | 3 | 15 | 12 | **15** |
| NORTHERN IRELAND | 10 | 2 | 3 | 5 | 10 | 18 | **9** |
| WALES | 10 | 2 | 2 | 6 | 10 | 15 | **8** |
| AZERBAIJAN | 10 | 0 | 3 | 7 | 1 | 21 | **3** |

### FINALS GROUP B

| | ENGLAND | Date | Venue |
|---|---|---|---|
| | **Paraguay** | 10 June | Frankfurt |
| | **Trinidad & Tobago** | 15 June | Nuremberg |
| | **Sweden** | 20 June | Cologne |

# David BECKHAM

## DON'T THINK WE'VE SEEN THE LAST OF 'GOLDEN-BALLS' YET – BECKHAM IS STILL ONE OF THE FEW MATCH-WINNING PLAYERS IN THE FINALS

He is the world's most recognisable sportsman, his image a carefully managed mix of family man, fashion model and smiling celebrity. But every now and then, a trademark stunning free-kick, a viciously curling cross or a pitch-length chase back to tackle will cut through all the fluff and remind us that the England captain is also one of the best footballers on the planet.

Now in his 30s, 'Becks' approaches the twilight of his career with a lorry load of memories already packed away. Back in 1996 his sensational goal from the halfway line against Wimbledon brought him to the nation's attention. By 1998, he finally forced his way into Glenn Hoddle's World Cup team, scoring against Colombia with a free-kick, only to be sent-off against Argentina for petulantly kicking-out.

By the 2002 World Cup qualifiers he was the captain, and with a captain's performance against Greece – including another fantastic free-kick – he single-handedly dragged England

'I think David Beckham is still one of the best players in the world. He's the best passer in the world and also one of the greatest players in his position on the pitch. I would love him to be Brazilian.'

Roberto Carlos

**FACT FILE** | MIDFIELD | 86 CAPS | 16 GOALS | REAL MADRID

Date of birth: **02.05.1975**
Height: **183 cm**
Weight: **74 kg**
Previous clubs: **Manchester United**
International debut: **01.09.1996 v Moldova**
Previous World Cups: **1998, 2002**

to the finals. Making it to the tournament despite a serious injury, he gained revenge on Argentina by scoring the penalty that beat them, but otherwise seemed out-of-sorts as England crashed out.

David Beckham has grown-up in public: winning the treble at Manchester United, his alleged bust-up with Alex Ferguson in the case of the flying boot and his high-profile transfer to Real Madrid. Trophies might have been elusive since he left for Spain, but the esteem in which he is held by the club and its fans leaves no doubt as to his contribution. Last season at Madrid, Beckham returned to the kind of form he showed at Manchester United. In contrast, although he continued to lead England with passion and exuberance, being moved from wing to centre to holding role seemed to dent his talents. He even handed his penalty-taking responsibility to Frank Lampard.

With his captaincy and even his place in the team under threat don't be surprised to see the usual Beckham reaction to adversity. He rolls up his sleeves, works even harder and pulls out a performance that leaves fans open-mouthed. This could well be his last World Cup, don't expect him to go out with a whimper.

*David Beckham has over 80 caps for England, the friendly against Argentina was his 50th match as captain.*

## STYLE GUIDE

⊕ 'Becks' is still England's talisman: at his best, his sheer energy is inspiring: a magnificent team player, he tracks back, launches himself into tackles and wants to take every free-kick or throw-in. England, if anything, take for granted his match-winning play from the right wing berth, complete with crossfield passes, curling pin-point crosses, buzz-bomb corners and, of course, awesome free-kicks.

# Wayne **ROONEY**

## HAVE ENGLAND FINALLY FOUND THAT SPECIAL TALENT THAT CAN TAKE THEM ALL THE WAY TO THE WORLD CUP FINAL?

Never before have England placed so much expectation on such a young talent. And yet, such is the power, dynamism and skill exhibited by the 20-year-old, that he too will face the world's finest, knowing that he could be the difference between his country's glory and failure.

'He can shoot from distance, get on the end of crosses, hit free-kicks – anything. He is someone who plays with absolutely no fear and when you have a striker like that then there are no limits.'

Thierry Henry

*Powerful and direct, Rooney has all the weapons to trouble the world's greatest defences.*

Wayne Rooney is no David Beckham. He lacks the good looks, the well-groomed image and film-star lifestyle, but he has the chance to be an even greater talisman for the national side. Ever since Everton's 17-year-old prodigy's scintillating shot passed the outstretched arms of Arsenal's David Seaman, England have believed they have found a Pelé or Maradona – a superstar who could take them right to the top.

Rooney quickly became England's youngest-ever player and goalscorer and at Euro 2004, he made a global impact not witnessed since Pelé in 1958. Having been man-of-the-match in all of England's group

**FACT FILE** | FORWARD | 28 CAPS | 11 GOALS | MANCHESTER UNITED

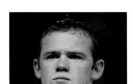

Date of birth: **24.10.1985**
Height: **178 cm**
Weight: **78 kg**
Previous clubs: **Everton**
International debut: **12.02.2003 v Australia**
Previous World Cups: **None**

games, he scared the living daylights out of the host nation, Portugal until, after 15 minutes, he limped off having broken a bone in his foot. England's tournament hopes soon followed.

Meanwhile, at home, 'Rooneymania' had taken root and the boy-turned-man found himself on his way from Goodison Park to Old Trafford. On his Champions League debut against Ferencvaros, Rooney scored a magnificent hat-trick, instantly justifying his £28 million fee. Superlatives kept coming as his performances electrified the Theatre of Dreams and gave England a cutting edge that seemed a million miles away when he was injured – or suspended.

Indeed, the wonderkid had an Achilles heel after all – his volatile temper. For club and country he would react to frustration with uncontrolled aggression. As some questioned his suitability, Rooney returned from international suspension to face Poland. He produced another thrilling man-of-the match performance, revitalising a moribund England and sending them to the top of their qualifying group. Suspect temper? Unsavoury private life? Perhaps: but without him England are champagne without the fizz – and who wants that?

**STYLE GUIDE**

⚽ When Rooney first hit the headlines, it was his powerful shooting, his incredible surging runs and boundless energy that won him accolades. Amazingly, the teenage prodigy added to his game – a superb positional sense, great vision and passing and an ability to animate his team-mates. Only his childlike reaction to frustrations belies his growing maturity.

# John **TERRY**

## ALREADY A CHELSEA LEGEND, THE IMMACULATE STOPPER HAS COME OF AGE FOR ENGLAND IN THE NICK OF TIME

**9 July 2006 – England skipper John Terry wipes a still sweating brow, pauses, and lifts high the World Cup. A far-fetched dream? Not any more. In England's final qualification match, a substituted Michael Owen handed the captain's armband to the Chelsea skipper. Terry's journey from England outcast to national leadership material was complete.**

*A series of inspirational performances for his club Chelsea during their championship winning season in 2004–05 have seen John Terry take his place as England's first-choice central defender.*

Among Chelsea's treasure trove of talent, John Terry stands alone as never having cost a penny. Yet, their home-grown hero can hold his own against any of the multi-million pound imports. Terry has been the spearhead of the Abramovich revolution: the mainstay of an impenetrable defence, the scorer of valuable goals and, most of all, an inspirational leader – Chelsea through and through.

Following a loan period at Gillingham, Terry got his break in the Chelsea side after an injury to Frank Leboeuf. As his replacement went from strength to strength, the World Cup winner never regained his place. When he was made club captain at the age of 23, Marcel Desailly dubbed Terry a 'Chelsea legend in the making', and Jose Mourinho was moved to call him the 'perfect player'. By the end of the 2004–05 season his fellow professionals seemed to agree, voting him the PFA Footballer of the Year.

Terry's England career was not keeping pace. An altercation with a night club bouncer left him with a court case pending. The FA, nervy after previous bad publicity, deferred his national call-up until the end of the case. Finally cleared of all offences, Terry made his belated debut against Serbia & Montenegro in 2003 – but there was still

**FACT FILE** | CENTRE-HALF | 21 CAPS | 0 GOALS | CHELSEA

Date of birth: **07.12.1980**
Height: **185 cm**
Weight: **88 kg**
Previous clubs: **None**
International debut: **03.06.2003 v Serbia & Montenegro**
Previous World Cups: **None**

## STYLE GUIDE

✪ Often compared to Tony Adams, the Chelsea stopper exerts his influence physically, verbally and by superb example. An immovable rock at the centre of the defence, Terry reads the game impeccably; he's powerful in the tackle, dominant in the air, and an ever-present attacking threat at free-kicks and corners.

'He is young but he has grown up. I hope I've taught him that off the pitch he has to be a leader.'

Marcel Desailly

the problem of Rio Ferdinand and Sol Campbell, a partnership that continued to live off the players' acclaimed performances in Japan and Korea.

Ferdinand's notorious suspension gave Terry his chance in time for Euro 2004, but playing with a hamstring injury, he failed to put in a permanent claim to the shirt. However, as Chelsea's championship season progressed, Terry's faultless performances, week after week, could not be ignored. By the autumn of 2005, Terry had become England's first-choice central defender, while Sol and Rio fought to partner him. Then came the armband and a snowballing press campaign to make him the full-time skipper.

# Frank LAMPARD

## HIS MANAGER THINKS HE'S THE BEST PLAYER IN EUROPE, AND IF HE PLAYS TO HIS POTENTIAL, LAMPS COULD LIGHT UP GERMANY

Heartbroken after narrowly missing the 2002 World Cup squad, the Chelsea midfielder was determined to make the plane next time round. In those four years, he's done more than that – he's become a Premiership winner, Footballer of the Year and an irreplaceable part of the England team.

Frank Lampard was never an ordinary player, but few believed he would make the progression to being a world-class midfielder. Now, through self-belief, great coaching and sheer hard work, he stands on the threshold of global recognition.

As the son of a Hammer hero, Frank began his career at West Ham – seemingly forever burdened with the suffix 'Junior'. There, alongside the likes of Rio Ferdinand, Joe Cole, and Michael Carrick, he impressed enough to make England Under-21 captain and

'The guy is simply a phenomenon. He never misses a game but doesn't look like he gets tired. Not just that, he was leading scorer for Chelsea in the Premiership last season. He inspires everyone around him.'

Sam Allardyce,

Bolton Wanderers manager

**FACT FILE** | MIDFIELD | 38 CAPS | 10 GOALS | CHELSEA

Date of birth: **20.06.1978**
Height: **183 cm**
Weight: **88 kg**
Previous clubs: **West Ham United**
International debut: **10.10.1999 v Belgium**
Previous World Cup: **None**

his debut in the senior side. But only when he left Upton Park and became *the* Frank Lampard did he really blossom.

In the early days at Stamford Bridge, Frank looked overweight and under-confident – his fee of £11 million rather extravagant. But under, first Ranieri, and then Mourinho, an altogether sharper player emerged. As more and more distinguished players joined the new 'Chelski', so Frank raised his game, daring his manager to leave him out. In the 2004–05 season he started in 58 games – and won the Footballer of the Year award.

Eriksson liked the look of the new slimline Frank, but he lost out in the final cut for Japan and Korea. By Euro 2004, however, he had established a settled place alongside Steven Gerrard, and emerged as one of England's stars of the tournament.

The qualifiers saw him impress further as a goalscoring midfielder, a natural successor to Paul Scholes. The only doubt was whether the presence of the similar forward-looking Gerrard limited Frank's game. While experts debated the point, Frank took over as penalty taker from Beckham, and carried on scoring.

## STYLE GUIDE

⚽ 'Lamps' is the epitome of the modern midfielder: he'll cover box to box all day long, his vision is stunning, his passing accurate and his tackling clinical. What takes him to another level is his incredible stamina and a stunning strike rate whether from his razor-sharp shooting, deadly free-kicks or penetrating runs from deep.

*Frank Lampard is regarded as one of the best midfielders in England. Next stop – the World Cup.*

# Michael OWEN

## THE NATION MAY HAVE A NEW TEENAGE HERO, BUT THE MATURE QUICKSILVER FORWARD IS STILL ENGLAND'S BABY-FACED ASSASSIN

If there is one team in the tournament who understand the true danger of Michael Owen it is Argentina. As a teenage prodigy, he took them on single-handedly; as an established international, he helped knock them out of the World Cup finals; and as a battle-worn forward, he nodded home two late goals to defeat them in the tense match in Geneva in November 2005.

Yet just a few months before that, unceremoniously dumped by Real Madrid, in poor form and overshadowed by the performances of new England idol Wayne Rooney, the No. 10 shirt he had owned for seven years looked under threat.

Owen had left Liverpool in August 2004 with nothing to prove. Consistently among the Premier League's top scorers, he helped Liverpool to the League Cup, FA Cup and UEFA Cup in 2001 and became the first British player for 20 years to win the European Footballer of the Year award. However, Liverpool's inability to make headway in the Champions League finally led to his move to Real Madrid for £8 million.

From being England's youngest ever scorer (a record now held by Rooney), Owen has grown up in the England team. After scoring as a substitute against Romania and netting the goal of the tournament against Argentina in the World Cup in 1998, he was an automatic selection. He became the only player to score in four major tournaments (the 1998 and 2002 World Cups and the 2000 and 2004 European Championships) for England and hit a hat-trick in the 5-1 victory over Germany in 2001. Established as Beckham's deputy captain, he became the youngest skipper

**FACT FILE** | FORWARD | 75 CAPS | 35 GOALS | NEWCASTLE UNITED

Date of birth: **14.12.1979**
Height: **175 cm**
Weight: **65 kg**
Previous clubs: **Real Madrid, Liverpool**
International debut: **11.02.1998 v Chile**
Previous World Cups: **1998, 2002**

since Bobby Moore in 2002 and regularly steps in if Beckham is absent.

Far from a disaster in Spain (he scored 13 goals with limited opportunities), Owen's return to the Premiership in 2005 – joining Newcastle United for £17 million – nevertheless rejuvenated the striker, though a broken toe in early 2006 might be a major setback.

No wonder England are smiling, once again, his pace, positional sense and lust for goals are clear to see. No defenders will be keen to see his name on England's teamsheet – least of all Argentina's.

## 'He's a great goalscorer, one of the best in the world. In the big games, he's always there and he's shown that for many years.'

Sven-Goran Eriksson

*Goals, goals, goals: Michael Owen is a typical striker, a predator who can appear uninterested in the game, then suddenly get on the end of a half-chance and score.*

**STYLE GUIDE**

⊕ The combination of raw pace, great positional sense and a clinical finish make Owen the complete forward. His international experience has seen his touch improve markedly and for such a short man he is lethal in the air. Some doubt his ablity to form a partnership with Rooney, but Owen is a natural goalscorer who can thrive on the creativity of his young team-mate.

# Steven **GERRARD**

**FACT FILE**

Position **Midfielder**

Caps **39**

Goals **6**

Club **Liverpool**

## HUNGRY FOR INTERNATIONAL SUCCESS

**One of the Premiership's most admired players, Steven Gerrard feels he still has it all to do at international level. Despite scoring in England's famous 5-1 victory over Germany in the qualifying rounds he missed out on the 2002 World Cup finals in Japan and Korea because of injury.**

Euro 2004 started badly for him when a disastrous backpass in the opening game against France went straight to Thierry Henry who was then brought down in the box by David James. Zinedine Zidane stepped up to fire home the winner. He never recovered his club form for England who went out in the quarter-finals after losing to Portugal on penalties.

A first-team regular since 1999–2000, Gerrard has played for Liverpool at every level since being spotted playing schoolboy football in Huyton aged eight. Prone to injuries in his early career, he has developed under the tutelage of Gérard Houllier and Sven-Goran Eriksson into a genuine world-class midfielder.

An inspirational player, Gerrard is at his best when driving forward in the centre of the pitch where, together with Frank Lampard, he now forms one of the most effective midfield units in the world. But England's strength in depth in this position coupled with Gerrard's ability to play anywhere often means that he is played out of position. That he doesn't mind, 'The team is more important than me and wherever the manager wants me to do a job, I'll do it to the best of my ability,' he says, speaks volumes for a player still hungry for success at the highest level.

# Joe **COLE**

**FACT FILE**
Position **Forward**
Caps **29**
Goals **4**
Club **Chelsea**

## FINALLY FULFILLING HIS POTENTIAL

**A star in the making since he joined the West Ham youth system, Joe Cole is finally coming of age for club and country. Now a regular starter in left midfield for Jose Mourinho at Chelsea, he is also the natural left-sided player that Sven-Goran Eriksson needs for the England midfield. Having made only one appearance, as a substitute in the 2002 World Cup and spending the whole of Euro 2004 on the bench, Cole is ready to take on the world's best in 2006.**

Long spoken about as the great hope of English football, Cole broke into the West Ham first-team in 1999– 2000 as a 17-year-old. He went on to make over 100 appearances for the club before they were relegated in 2003 and then made the move to Chelsea.

He didn't really flourish in his first season at Stamford Bridge under manager Claudio Ranieri. But the arrival of Jose Mourinho changed everything. 'I'm a link man, playing behind the strikers,' says Cole, 'and that man [Mourinho] is the first manager who has come in and played me in my right position.' Mourinho is famed for his abilities as a man-manager, and a few choice words of criticism, delivered at the right time – such as after his winning goal at Anfield on New Year's Day 2004 – after which Chelsea embarked on their Premiership-winning run, are invaluable to a confidence player like Joe Cole.

His maturing play has brought a regular place in the international team. Though right-footed, Cole has the skills and vision to play on the left side of midfield, can run at defenders and beat them, has the ability to make defence-splitting passes and can score goals too. The World Cup in 2006 will present Joe Cole with his biggest challenge yet. England fans are confident that he will rise to it and finally fulfil his huge potential.

# Paul ROBINSON

**FACT FILE**

Position **Goalkeeper**

Caps **18**

Goals **0**

Club **Tottenham Hotspur**

## AGILE SHOT-STOPPER GETTING RAVE REVIEWS

Picked for the England Under-21 side while at Leeds, Paul Robinson has long had the potential to be England's No.1. But he had to wait until September 2004 to be given a regular place in the senior team when he replaced David James after a poor performance against Austria.

Since then Robinson has impressed everyone with his consistency and confidence. He made a memorable save to deny John Hartson's point-blank header against Wales in the World Cup qualifier and then put in a magnificent all-round performance in the friendly against Argentina in November 2005 to cement his place between the sticks.

Signed by Leeds United in 1993 at the age of 14, Paul Robinson worked his way up to the senior team and was regularly vying for the keeper's jersey with Nigel Martyn during the Yorkshire side's Champions League adventures in 2000–01. When Martyn left for Everton in 2002 Robinson proved a reliable replacement and was soon a regular part of the England squad.

Leeds were relegated at the end of the 2003–04 season and he made a much-anticipated move to Spurs. His form for both club and country has remained superb since then earning praise from the likes of England legend and goalkeeping coach Ray Clemence, 'If a team and a defence feels they've got a goalkeeper behind them who is going to make great saves like he does ... then it helps to breed confidence in everybody.' Judging by Robinson's performances during the qualifying matches, England might at last have found a worthy replacement for David 'safe hands' Seaman.

# Ashley **COLE**

**FACT FILE**

Position **Defender**
Caps **44**
Goals **0**
Club **Arsenal**

## A PERFECT MIX OF YOUTH AND EXPERIENCE

**Despite a wretched first half of the 2005–06 season, during which he was sidelined for two months with a stress fracture of the foot, Ashley Cole is sure to be England's left back in Germany 2006. Already one of England's finest defenders, still only 25, Cole is also hugely experienced playing a full part in both the 2002 World Cup and Euro 2004 campaigns.**

A product of the Arsenal youth scheme, Cole first played as a striker. He made his senior club debut up front in a League Cup match against Middlesbrough in 1999. But his first-team chances were limited with Dennis Bergkamp, Thierry Henry, Kanu and Davor Suker all competing for places. A loan spell at Crystal Palace followed in 2000 but an injury to the Gunners' Brazilian full back Silvinho resulted in manager Arsène Wenger giving Cole his chance and he took it with both hands.

His pace and his timing in the tackle saw Cole slip seamlessly into the Arsenal back four and his attacking instincts gave the team an extra dimension. Rewarded for his club form, Cole made his debut on the international stage against Albania in March 2001 and he has been a regular ever since. Sometimes criticised for his temperament and sometimes for neglecting his defensive duties, Cole's electric pace often allows him time to recover, he provides a natural outlet on the left and is able to turn defence into attack at lightning speed.

With over 150 Premiership appearances and 50 Champions League games for Arsenal and 44 England caps, Ashley Cole's experience is invaluable at the top level and has made him an integral part of Sven-Goran Eriksson's team.

# Rio FERDINAND

**FACT FILE**

Position **Defender**

Caps **44**

Goals **1**

Club **Manchester United**

## ELEGANT DEFENDER WITH MUCH TO PROVE

**The jury is out on Rio Ferdinand. Some, like Harry Redknapp, can't praise him enough, 'He's a Rolls Royce of a defender,' says his former manager. Others, current manager Sir Alex Ferguson among them, seem to think that sometimes his mind is not on the job in hand.**

He joined West Ham from school in 1992, made his first-team debut four years later. His first international cap came in 1997 and in 2000 he became the British record transfer when he joined Leeds for £18 million. In 2002 he partnered Sol Campbell in central defence for England in the World Cup where he put in some tremendous performances. He was so impressive that Sir Alex Ferguson then spent £30 million to take him to Old Trafford and in his first season he was part of the championship-winning team.

Things started to go wrong on 23 September 2003 when he 'failed' to turn up for a random drugs test after a league match against Arsenal. He was subsequently banned from all football for eight months including England's Euro 2004 campaign.

Many critics think that he has failed to recapture his form since returning from his ban and protracted contract negotiations at Old Trafford did not help his profile among the fans. Poor club performances in the early part of the 2005–06 season saw him substituted regularly. Though he was given his place back in England's central defence for the qualifiers, his poor club form saw him dropped to the bench for the final two games. Rio Ferdinand has much to prove.

# Luke **YOUNG**

**FACT FILE**
Position **Defender**
Caps **7**
Goals **0**
Club **Charlton Athletic**

## PUSHING FOR A FIRST-TEAM BERTH

**First capped for England in the summer of 2005 on England's tour to the USA as a replacement for the injured Gary Neville, many people feel that he has done enough to keep the job for the World Cup in 2006.**

The six-foot defender started his career at White Hart Lane playing full back and central defence. Though he was a regular member of the first-team his appearances were limited by the presence of Stephen Carr, and in July 2001, having made over 70 appearances for Spurs, he joined Charlton Athletic for £3 million.

Installed immediately at right back, his progress at the Valley under manager Alan Curbishley has been rapid. He suffered a setback when he missed much of the 2003–04 season through injury, but he only missed two games the following season, was Charlton's player of the year and was rewarded with a place in the England squad for his efforts. Initially used by Sven-Goran Eriksson as a substitute, he got his first start in the World Cup qualifier against Wales and retained his place for the remaining matches as well as the friendly against Argentina in November.

Energetic and tough in the tackle, Young is also good at getting forward in support of the attack and is capable of firing in dangerous crosses. Though it seems likely that Gary Neville will be the first choice at right back, he has yet to prove his fitness, even at club level. What is certain is that Luke Young will be pushing him for a place all the way to Germany.

# Gary NEVILLE

**FACT FILE**

Position **Defender**

Caps **77**

Goals **0**

Club **Manchester United**

## MR RELIABLE OUT TO PROVE HIS WORTH

**A more committed player than Gary Neville is hard to find. A one-club man at Manchester United, Gary is also fiercely proud of his place in the England team and his never-say-die attitude is an inspiration to team-mates and England fans alike. Injuries permitting Gary Neville will give more than his fair share of blood, sweat and tears for the England cause in Germany 2006.**

Signed by United as a 16-year-old trainee in 1991, Gary Neville has plied his trade as right back (and sometimes central defender) in over 400 matches for the Red Devils. Rewarded for his club performances with an international call-up in 1995, Neville has played a major role for England in four major tournaments since then, only missing out in the 2002 World Cup because of injury.

Pacy and aggressive, Neville is a reliable defender, while his link-up play with former team-mate David Beckham has been a factor in the England team's successes in the last few years. Recent absences through injury have shown the England defence to be weaker without him. A noisy player on the pitch, continually geeing up his team-mates, Gary is also to be heard off it, representing the players to the management when things don't go smoothly and is mentioned as a possible future chairman of the PFA (Professional Footballers' Association).

However, now 31 Neville is more prone to injury. He missed the World Cup qualifiers with a groin injury and will have to work hard on his match fitness before the summer of 2006. Hugely important to the England cause, Neville's attitude and aggression will be sorely missed if he does not make it.

# Sol **CAMPBELL**

**FACT FILE**

Position **Defender**

Caps **66**

Goals **1**

Club **Arsenal**

## EXPERIENCED DEFENDER CRUCIAL TO ENGLAND

**A reassuring presence at the heart of the defence, Sol Campbell is one of the most experienced players in the England team. The World Cup in 2006 will be his sixth major tournament. Tall, powerful, commanding in the air, a good distributor of the ball and a thrilling sight carrying the ball forward at pace, Campbell could be a major factor in England's progress.**

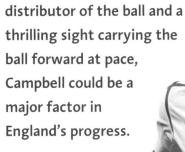

Campbell joined Tottenham as a schoolboy, making his first-team debut in 1992. During the next few years he became the mainstay of the Spurs team gradually replacing club captain Gary Mabbutt in central defence. He was called up for England duty in the warm-up games for Euro 96 and even started in the famous victory against Scotland at Wembley later that year. He played a major part in England's World Cup campaign in 1998 and in the European Championships in 2000.

In 2001, a landmark year for the player, he stunned everyone by moving to Spurs arch rivals Arsenal. Despite the furore, Campbell continued to play his best football and quickly settled in at Highbury. His performances for England, alongside Rio Ferdinand, at the World Cup in 2002 – during which he scored his only international goal against Sweden – earned him plaudits and a place in the FIFA team of the tournament.

He played his part in Arsenal's fabulous unbeaten season in 2003–04 and in England's efforts at Euro 2004 in Portugal. However, 2005 was not a good year for him as a succession of injuries: from hamstring, to Achilles, to calf, to ankle, have severely restricted his appearances for Arsenal. Despite these setbacks, Campbell's power, presence and experience make him invaluable for the World Cup in 2006.

# Ledley **KING**

**FACT FILE**
Position **Defender**
Caps **15**
Goals **1**
Club **Tottenham Hotspur**

## GREAT FORM GIVES SVEN PROBLEMS

King's first-team career started slowly at Tottenham as a series of injuries and the presence of Sol Campbell restricted his appearances. But when Campbell left for Arsenal in 2001 King became the rock at the heart of the Spurs defence. Strong, able to tackle and a commanding presence at the back, King was awarded his first England cap in 2002. He appeared irregularly for the national side for the next two years until a series of injuries to first-choice defenders saw him start against France in England's opening match at Euro 2004.

Despite doubts among fans and punters, King put in a marvellous performance under pressure. His calmness and poise, which are such a feature of his game, have since made him central to Sven-Goran Eriksson's plans for the World Cup in Germany.

King is also a versatile player, having played in midfield as well as central defence during his early career, and when England hit a bad patch during 2005 Sven-Goran Eriksson decided to play 4-5-1 rather than the usual 4-4-2 with King as the holding player. Though the experiment was not a great success in terms of results, King's performances in the new formation were a revelation. The World Cup in Germany will present King with the chance to test himself against the world's best attackers.

# Jamie **CARRAGHER**

**FACT FILE**

Position **Defender**

Caps **22**

Goals **0**

Club **Liverpool**

## ALL-ACTION DEFENDER FLYING THE FLAG

A product of the famous Liverpool Academy, Jamie Carragher has established a reputation as a fine defender, an effective man-marker and someone prepared to give everything for the cause. His performances for Liverpool during the Champions League-winning campaign in 2004–05 saw him write himself into the club's folklore.

Jamie Carragher made his Premiership debut for Liverpool in 1996–97. Since then he has clocked up well over 300 first-team appearances in the Reds' rearguard. Although a specialist defender, Carragher has played in virtually every position, whether left or right full back, central defender or wing back. It is not really clear what his best position is but what is clear is that he is one of England's most natural defenders.

Since making his England debut against Hungary in 1999 he has not always featured regularly. He was not selected for Euro 2000, missed the 2002 World Cup through injury and though he was in the squad for Euro 2004 he didn't get off the bench during the tournament. However, his defensive talents were well illustrated during 2004–05 when he appeared in every one of Liverpool's Premier League matches and played superbly as the Reds became European Champions for the fifth time in their history overcoming AC Milan in the Final having been 3-0 down at half-time.

Carragher is a crowd favourite for both club and country, a player whose attitude ensures that he always gives 100 per cent, and that's exactly what Sven-Goran Eriksson will need from his players if they're to lift the trophy in Berlin on 9 July.

## David **JAMES**

Position **Goalkeeper**    Caps **33**    Goals **0**
Club **Manchester City**

Became England's No. 1 on David Seaman's retirement after the 2002 World Cup. A big man, brave and an excellent shot stopper. Played well in Euro 2004 but was increasingly prone to errors and was replaced in 2005 by Paul Robinson. Good form for his club earned him a recall to the squad later in the year.

## Robert **GREEN**

Position **Goalkeeper**    Caps **1**    Goals **0**
Club **Norwich City**

Highly rated and agile for a big man, Robert Green was called up by Sven-Goran Eriksson for the friendly against Sweden in 2004 and finally made his debut on England's tour of the United States the following year. Has kept his place in the squad despite his club, Norwich City, being relegated from the Premiership.

## Wayne **BRIDGE**

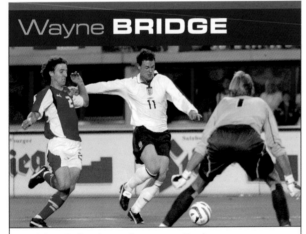

Position **Defender**    Caps **21**    Goals **1**
Club **Chelsea**

Cultured defender, who now plays his club football with Chelsea, Bridge missed much of their 2004–05 championship-winning season with a broken leg. Naturally left-footed, he likes to get forward and can deliver pin-point crosses. Appeared during the 2002 World Cup and was in the squad for Euro 2004.

## Paul **KONCHESKY**

Position **Defender**    Caps **2**    Goals **0**
Club **West Ham United**

A left-sided defender, Paul Konchesky was first called up as a midfielder for the friendly against Australia in February 2003 but did not gain his second cap until October 2005. Strong on the ball, able to move forward at speed, he is also a fine crosser of the ball. Joined West Ham from Charlton in 2005 where he now plays at left back.

## Jermaine JENAS

Position **Midfielder**    Caps **14**    Goals **0**
Club **Tottenham Hotspur**

A cultured midfielder, Jenas joined Newcastle from Nottingham Forest for £5 million in 2002. He moved again in 2005, this time to Spurs. A regular in the England set-up since early 2003 Jenas is renowned for his energetic play and for spectacular goals from outside the box. Still young, Jenas is a big hope for Germany 2006.

## Michael CARRICK

Position **Midfielder**    Caps **4**    Goals **0**
Club **Tottenham Hotspur**

Carrick is a candidate for the holding role in Sven's starting line-up in Germany. He made his senior international debut against Mexico in 2001 as a West Ham player. Moved to Spurs for £4 million in 2004. Calm under pressure, composed on the ball, Carrick is a ball winner and one of the finest passers in the Premiership.

## Jermain DEFOE

Position **Forward**    Caps **15**    Goals **1**
Club **Tottenham Hotspur**

Lively, quick-footed striker, joined Tottenham from West Ham in January 2004. He has been a regular member of the England squad since his move to North London but has rarely been in the starting line-up. However, his pace and eye for goal at club level mean that Sven-Goran Eriksson might turn to him at any time.

## Peter CROUCH

Position **Forward**    Caps **4**    Goals **0**
Club **Liverpool**

Tall and lanky, Crouch is particularly good on the ground. He signed for Liverpool in 2005 two months after he made his international debut on England's summer tour to the USA. His height – 6 foot 7 inches – makes him an alternative target man for the midfield and a useful squad player for the England coach.

# ENGLAND'S PROSPECTS

**All the hype aside, and there will be plenty of it before the tournament starts, England have their best chance since 1966 to win football's greatest tournament. The Premier League is stronger than ever and with players like Wayne Rooney, Frank Lampard, Steven Gerrard, John Terry, Ashley Cole and Joe Cole, England have a genuine world-class XI.**

England have been drawn in Group B with Paraguay, Trinidad & Tobago and Sweden. Manager Sven Goran-Eriksson was pleased with the draw, even though it pits his newly adopted country against his own nation, again! 'It is not an easy group but it could have been much worse,' he said with customary understatement. On current form, England should get through to the second round, but both Paraguay, who they play on 10 June in Frankfurt, and Sweden will be tough to beat.

## OLD FRIENDS, OLD ENEMIES

Paraguay have an ageing but experienced defence and will rely on their natural attacking tendencies. These skills enabled them to beat tournament favourites Argentina during the notoriously difficult South American qualifying tournament in which Paraguay finished fourth. Up front they have two hungry young strikers, Roque Santa Cruz and Nelson Haedo Valdez, who both ply their trade in the Bundesliga. England should win their encounter but this opening match will be a stern test of their mettle.

The second match, on 15 June, is against outsiders Trinidad & Tobago, the lowest ranked team in the competition. Though England must win the match if they're going to win the group it's sure to be a fabulous occasion as two of the noisiest sets of fans get together in Nuremberg. Old friends will be reunited during the encounter when current and former Premiership players Shaka Hislop, Stern John and former Manchester United favourite Dwight Yorke take to the field for the Caribbean team.

The final group match against Sweden in Cologne on 20 June, is the toughest. England have not beaten the Scandinavian side in 39 years. The two teams drew 1-1 in their opening match of the World Cup in 2002 and Sweden won 1-0 in 2004 – their only encounter since then. Solid at the back and dangerous up front England may well struggle if they have to win to qualify. In Zlatan Ibrahimovic and Henrik Larsson, Sweden have two of the most exciting strikers in the world as well as Premiership regular Freddie Ljungberg. However, England fans will be hoping that the team has already qualified by then and that will take the pressure off.

## GETTING SERIOUS

Once the knockout rounds begin, the draw is in two parts, which means that teams from the top half will not meet teams from the bottom half until the Final. This means that should England qualify, and they certainly should, then they will avoid the Czech Republic, Italy, Brazil, France and Spain. If they win the group then they will probably meet Costa Rica or Poland in the second round and Holland or Argentina in the quarter-finals. If they finish second, then things might get serious immediately with a match against the winners of Group A which is likely to be hosts Germany.

Of course, to win the World Cup you have to beat everybody and inevitably that means beating either Argentina or Brazil, or both. If England avoid injuries to key players, hit form early and come up with a Plan B, Germany 2006 could represent their best chance of winning football's biggest prize.